The Pump Monster

by Susan Gates
illustrated by Laura Sua

CAMBRIDGE
UNIVERSITY PRESS

UCL
Institute of Education

Hanna grew a big pumpkin.
She was very happy with it.

Everyone in the town came to see it.

'That's the biggest pumpkin we have ever seen!' they said.

Hanna's pumpkin grew bigger
and bigger until it was a monster!

Now everyone was scared.

'Get rid of that pumpkin,'
they said to Hanna.

'I want food!'
shouted the Pumpkin Monster.

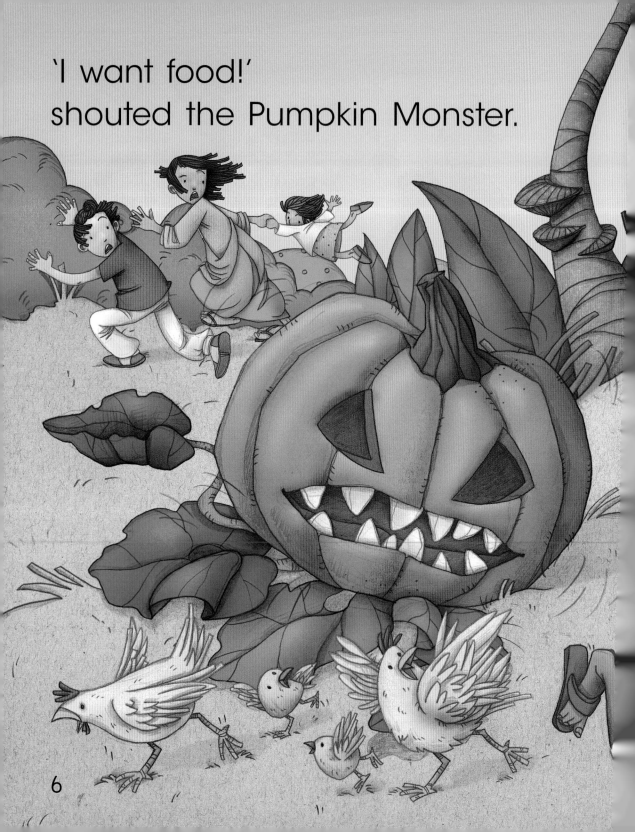

And it rolled away, looking for things to eat.

Hanna ran after
the Pumpkin Monster.

It rolled into a field of corn and gobbled it all up.

Soon the Pumpkin Monster was as big as a house.

'Stop eating our corn,' said Hanna, 'or we will be hungry!'

But the monster did not
stop eating.

'I want food!' it shouted
and rolled on and on.

Hanna chased
the Pumpkin Monster into a forest.

It rolled over some trees
with sharp thorns.

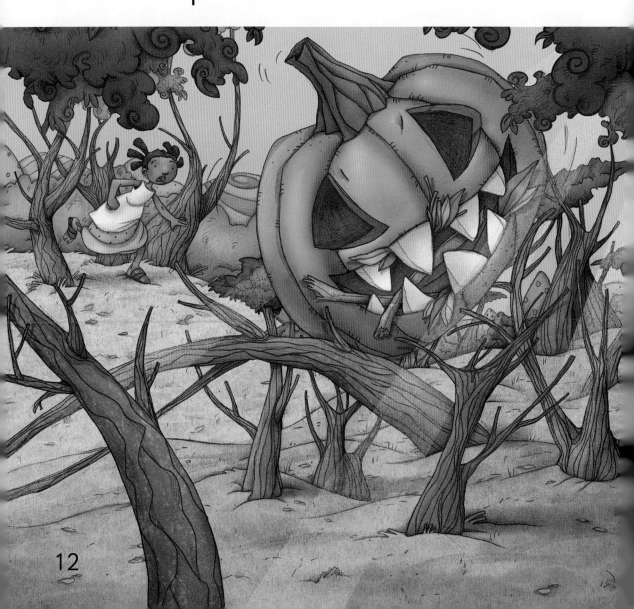

'PSST!' went the monster.
'Pssssssssst.'

The Pumpkin Monster got
smaller and smaller.

Soon, the Pumpkin Monster
was like a little orange puddle.

'The Pumpkin Monster has gone,'
said Hanna.

'Now we will not be hungry!'

'Hurray for Hanna!' said everyone.

The Pumpkin Monster 🐡 Susan Gates

Teaching notes written by Sue Bodman and Glen Franklin

Using this book

Developing reading comprehension

This tale follows a familiar cumulative story framework, such as that used in 'The Gingerbread Man'. A pumpkin grows bigger and bigger until it becomes a monster, but Hanna saves the day and the pumpkin gets his comeuppance. Levels of inference are required, for example making the causal link between the sharp thorns and the deflated monster.

Grammar and sentence structure

- Sentences vary in length, for example, longer sentences separated by a reporting clause to build suspense: 'Stop eating our corn,' said Hanna, 'or we will be hungry.' (page 10).
- Use of literary language ('as big as a house') and repeated phrases ('I want food!').
- Complex sentences including adverbial phrases, such as 'Hanna chased the pumpkin into a forest.' (page 12).

Word meaning and spelling

- Use of onomatopoeia ('Pssssssst' on page 13) to describe the pumpkin deflating.
- Comparative and superlative adjectives ('big', 'bigger and bigger', 'biggest') are used to demonstrate the growth of the pumpkin.

Curriculum links

Science – Projects on growing, such as children planting their own pumpkin seeds. Whose pumpkin will grow the biggest?

History – Hanna is very brave. Use non-fiction books and the internet to look for true life stories of heroines in your context.

Learning outcomes

Children can:

- comment on events and characters, using the text to support their opinions
- monitor their own errors and show a greater degree of self-correction
- demonstrate automatic recall of known high frequency words.

A guided reading lesson

Book Introduction

Give each child a copy of the book. Read the title and the blurb with them. Ask them to do a slow check of the words 'monster´ and 'pumpkin' by running their finger under the word and saying the sounds slowly. Check children all know what a pumpkin is. Ask the children to predict what the story will be about, using the information from the blurb and the illustrations on the front and back cover.

Orientation

Give a brief overview of the story, using the same verb tense as used in the book, In this story, Hanna's pumpkin grew into a monster and the villagers were really scared. They wanted Hanna to help them. I wonder if she is brave enough – what do you think?

Preparation

Page 2: Discuss what is happening on this page, introducing Hanna. Ask: 'Why do you think she was happy with her pumpkin?' Explore the difference between the word 'big' on page 2 and 'biggest' on page 3, drawing attention to the doubled consonant. Practice saying the line 'That's the biggest pumpkin we have ever seen!' with expression.

Page 4: Note the literary phrase 'bigger and bigger.' rehearsing how this would